PETROGLYPHS

Poems by
Fred Ostrander

BLUE LIGHT PRESS ◆ 1ST WORLD PUBLISHING

1st WORLD
PUBLISHING

SAN FRANCISCO ◆ FAIRFIELD ◆ DELHI

PETROGLYPHS

Copyright ©2009 by Fred Ostrander

1ST WORLD PUBLISHING
106 South Court Street
Fairfield, Iowa 52556
www.1stworldpublishing.com

BLUE LIGHT PRESS
1563 45th Avenue
San Francisco, California, 94122

AUTHOR
ostrand7@pacbell.net
2630 Saklan Indian Drive #3
Walnut Creek, CA 94595
925-930-9524

COVER PHOTO
Kenneth Ingham

BOOK DESIGN
Melanie Gendron
www.melaniegendron.com

FIRST EDITION

LCCN: 2009932365

ISBN: 978-1-4218-9111-8

To Nancy

ACKNOWLEDGEMENTS

Some of these poems have appeared in the following journals and publications:

Asheville Poetry Review, Baltimore Review, Blue Unicorn, Crucible Literary Journal, Drumvoices Review, Eclipse, Epicenter, Eureka Literary Magazine, Hampden-Sydney Poetry Review, Hawaii Review, Hawaii Pacific Review, Iodine Poetry Journal, Meridian Anthology of Contemporary Poetry, Nimrod International Journal, Permafrost, Poem: A Literary Journal, Poetry International, Phantasmagoria, Porcupine Literary Arts Magazine, REAL: A Literary Journal, Rattlesnake Review, Sanskrit Review, Seventh Quarry, Sierra-Nevada College Review, Southern Poetry Review, Sulphur River Literary Review, Texas Review, West Wind Review, Willow Review, Wisconsin Review, Zone 3, others

I would also like to acknowledge the editorial assistance of Lawrence Hart and of John Hart, poet, teacher, writer, environmentalist, friend.

CONTENTS

6: HOW IT INCREASES

7: THE FLIGHT OF THE MONARCH

ABOUT THE AUTHOR

TO SELECT FROM A LIFETIME

To select from a lifetime moments and reminders
of a life, your years, would take another life
and time would double,
and the time full of ancestors that selectively narrowed to you.

So I will not mention those moments
so briefly experienced
that for no reason are deeply important.
How, for example near Camp Meeker,
we watched sheep moving through the fog
on the road to the ocean.
Or when we watched the blackbirds, the many thousands,
rise from the field
and return to the field.
The rainbow that glowed and shone
against the darkness of the mountains.
Or when, in the Himalayas,
we walked and climbed to the crag
to watch the sunrise,
that granite place,
and light complete the sky.

Nor will I mention
the green, placid, gleaming
drifting, river Nile
between monuments of such great beauty and command
like visible archetypes
and we realize how limited is our imagination.
And the Valley of the Kings
and the passages down
to the place of the Pharaoh, his eternal room.

The gold mask over the wrinkled, not living face
taken by robbers at some point
during the last three thousand years.
His room with the perfectly detailed paintings upon the walls
of herons, water-plants, snakes
and a procession of dog-headed and bird-headed gods
and the ceiling bright with the many stars
and that thin bright boat the new god
will row into the stars.

Where we have camped
the stars crossed the skies above us
like an immense riddle
a riddle not of language
and only solved in those rare moments, briefly,
and the answer is erased
and the skies remain unsolved.

A lifetime of love and joy eludes many.
But there are those moments, you said,
when eyes meet other eyes
and the understanding expands beyond
the restrictions that follow us
like censors with their pencils.
And the joy grows from the heart
into all of time, and for the moment,
love is known, and for the moment, is forever.

Nancy, there is an irrational ferocity,
a psychopathic fury
that is spreading everywhere upon this planet.
We have seen the reptiles flying low to the sand
with great, slowly beating wings.

2

The black headlines in the paper rack.
The garish colors in the television window
assemble into monstrous scenes. Think
of Goya and his dark sketches.
The snake slides from the tree with flickering tongue.
Predatory eyes and eyes filled with terror.
Nancy, your grace, gentleness, your eyes that so far
can show to our human fear,
hope, love, intellect that can understand . . .

There is an unremitting rhythm that includes us all, I think,
the brain-mind, the heart, our great lungs, sex, binocular eyes, all,
and the mechanical skeleton with the loose shelves,
the various evolutionary distributions
of bones, the grimaces, the beatific smile,
a structure that can walk, climb, fall, break
upon the paved directions.
Or perhaps it is part of the scheme
plotted by the small wrinkled figure
crouched beside the edge of the sea
staring at stars.

I will not take the time to describe the scene of our meeting,
that night, the thin, fragmenting clouds drifting
blue and iridescent past the moon,
the surf, shallow, folding at the very edge
followed by the great beautiful breakers.

We walked the length of those eternal sands.

1

THE WORD

THE WORD

It is always there, if I wait.
The immense cloud-shadow moving across the far mountains.
The streak of a tanager in the dark trees,
the green spiraling and unspiraling snake
the fish in the rapids, the bear who dazzles the stream,
the voluble coyotes coming down beneath the moon.

It lasts for a moment, this reassembly of the self,
an identity that we believe for a moment is ours,
as the petrel over the high-breaking seas;
the eagle, his great slow wingspread, returning to the cliff,
or the high-pitched repeated cry of the hawk, the brilliance
of sun through the splayed wing-feathers, drifting across.

And you, grandfather, long since passed into the matter
of the wind, little remains of the singing that you followed.
A different creation, another legend.
A stone fallen out of a star-dense sky.

I hear the word
in the approaching, ancient silence, the name in the forgetting,
watching the pattern of the wind shimmering the river
waiting perhaps for centuries for a particular moment
for the completion of a star in its incalculable circling

Like a word that, ignored, appears for a moment and returns,
lucid, to the circle of our reaching,
the radius of our love.

ANCESTORS

Photographs, dark, scratched, in impractical frames
that give the appearance of wreaths
out of which stare for an instant
the brave, the frightened, the captured—
who dreamed, with little sleep
as a great wind moves across the dark grasses of a country of horses
across a moonlight without roads.

Rachel with great bones, Sarah like a petal upon the table,
John difficult to make out beneath the scratches,
Constance, Aby, Jasper. They remain
as a momentary, yellowing and unrepeatable image,
an instant in which they were taken and cannot change.
They stare with uncertainty, distrust even,
the unrecognition of the survivor coming out of the snow.

What deaths account for these eyes?
The visceral terror upon reaching the limits of their journey
beneath the wooden letters eroding in the plains-wind . . .

Four births—three deaths
in the wagons—against the snow-wind
or beneath the distortions of the blue-brilliant sun
that alters the expression upon the permanent face—
jaw and hollow and wanting—
and the eye's glint against the mountains.

Fathers cross the shadows like migrants—
the great hands of mothers—
aunts falling away into the past
loosened from the actual as by a wind—
Gladys under the moon.

From doors they were not intended to leave
into lands they were not intended to enter
a field where the stars are dense, the stone unusual.

I look back after the great interval.
It is here that the trail enters the trees
and the memory is very far, and small, and shining—
as a waltz upon a floor—as a stone transferred between hands—
as a threshold
upon which one stood through the generations of the snow.

GRANDFATHER

Wanderer of an extreme age, speaking a previous language,
Grandfather,
the Nevada mountains are visible to me,
and the small, indecisive birds in the willows who speak incessantly,
and the path into the vertical rocks.
The lightning illuminates, briefly, the Sierra, mountain, and mountain.
The forgotten people, the Paiutes, and before them,
drifting across the valley, living behind trees,
along creeks, in the crumbling cliffs, in the farthest range.

And I speak to you, in this suspended moment,
who will not return to the petals of the desert
mechanically opening,
that appear after the downpour, the flood in the swale.
The blue iridescent blackbirds, returning to the fields
and the white, abstract, jangling flowers.

Some instant of light, from before time,
crosses all of the immeasurably vast, completely black space,
arrives upon a small, blue and solitary, alternating eye.

How is it I am able to accompany you?
I continue to call, to listen for you,
door after opening door, where you might appear
in some last room—
as in the instant when a dream
is remembered, lifting you upon some rising, resistless river.

I stare across the sands where I have walked
stars visible by daylight, beneath the circle of the sky
in the stammering delirium, where others shout
and gesture impatiently. The hidden is found.
Whom you listen for, replies.

SPEAKING TO MY SISTER

All that I have left unfinished, among the black windows,
the spider at its trickery, the moonlight upon the room's disorder . . .

What is the legend that created us? You. And me.
Our Gothic years.
The fingers of the spinner working at their threads,
the unprotected cradle, misidentification and mistake.
And the moon makes its progress past the attic window,
intimating this.

The past is immediate and I am secret.
It was you who reached the turning, the dark, interrupting trees.
You were and in the instant that followed were not.
Removed into the rooms of a dream.

     Dear S.,
When did the search for the explanation become
an Escher-like repeated staircase?
Was it my inability to reach toward you into unexplained
        directions,
the dark sea-painting hanging from the nail?

Figures fall to pieces in the grass like statues,
the plaster, astonished faces.
Great eyes upon the verge of darkness.
And the transient remembers the eternal room.

IT IS NOT MINE

It is not mine, that I have received,
the moon impermanent and unwithheld.

I reconvey the fear beyond my fear.
It is no longer mine that I received.

And I that lived am forfeit to that other,
the face that I have pledged for all I own.

And I that loved will be the stranger soon,
the death I wake upon without a word.

I falter to approach, not to resist
an iris in eclipse and all that shone.

And I that loved am forfeit thereby, father,
and walk among the phantoms I project.

So I turn and reach where you stare back
and all that I have taken now I offer.

THE BIRD

We drive in silence, the streetlight shining
through the rain, upon the windshield, like a rose.
Midnight, obligations, calendars, pulling us apart.
The airplane lights are lifting through the rain.

There was a street we could not find again,
the great wind tearing the signs off the brackets, the shops,
sellers among their shelves.
In the darkness of the taxidermist's cabinets,
the small, stationary, iridescent bird was mounted like a ruby
in the position of flight—

Could we have known how rapidly it passes?

A heart is glowing like a cup in the dark street,
crooked arms reaching out of the shawls, unsorted faces.
The rain is falling upon the parking asphalt,
the cars starting up, a garish rain about the lighted lettering,
and I feel a change of fear, a revision of verbs.

DAWN

A swallow is swinging out from the cliffs. I wake
into the beginning. The dawn is yellow like a great leaf
over the dark graph of mountains, and a further, pale, lifted and luminous
range.
The bats are flocking back into the cliff. Overhead,
huge and windy, a Catholic cloud, chaotic, gold, baroque,
and the wind among the swifts
shimmers the grasses and the reflections of the grasses.
I stand beside the pond, looking in. I am alone.

I cannot withstand
the images, one pushing upon the other, in my distractions.
In my skin exists the frail fossil man,
the head bent heavily
over the charts, itineraries,
and a remote understanding that is growing into definition.

In the pond, a few pollywogs twist and wiggle like commas.
Insects float and glitter in the circles. I do not know
what will follow. A not inevitable consequence
of events I cannot rescind
and that continue into the past, like diminishing hands.

I wade into the pond, the center of great circles.
The chill encroaches
upon my skin and eyes.

SUNSET

Below us the cliff sways, the wind,
the surf returns and mingles among the little shells,
wings and lamps,
the kelp and the iodine.

Our faces, altered with the dusk,
turn in the one direction,
jacket over the ribs,
the heart new as a seed.

Elbows pressed into the plants
among the Monarchs, the grasses,
legs, arms, variously bent, older,
existence tugging within the chest,
eyes shifting from the other to the sea.

The enormous, ignited, illuminated sky
dominating us, the sun going down
into the shadows,
Ixion burning.

Remember, the black road through the headland,
our lights shone into the crickets,
in our eyes the isolation and the long breakers
and the heart's single, small direction
red as a sail.

2

I Write to You

SONG

That afternoon we walked across those fields—remember
there was a wind—the bees were clinging to the stamens—
the cumulus crossing, abolishing blue—
upon impulse we went down to the lake
pushed the boat out beyond the clogging, floating leaves
(it is always half-sinking and you have to bail)
and I remember the sound of the oars, and the wings of ducks
beating and lifting against the water in their effort to rise . . .

It was after, the dusk glimmering into the leaves of the path,
that we walked again beneath them: the stars: Orion overhead.
They shone, they were gold, as if in a wind,
configurations of ships, and animals with wings,
and I remembered or saw once again
with a vividness I cannot ascribe to memory
the tree you led me to: it illuminated all of that November.
And your ghost congruent with those intricate branches
and the singers in the branches and the wild sparrow . . .

And all night now I drive toward you, the double lights
upon the paving, the superb eyes
of animals beside the road, but you are not in this geography.
I call out
that you may reappear, but if I reach to you
extending all of my fingers, you will reappear
in another room, at another distance, upon another branch
and I must again adjust my focus, my direction
searching for the dimension in which I may locate you,
in what bright dimension I may locate you.

Oh my love, do you not understand? In the traffic intersections, the injuries, in the vegetable shops with the leaves and the great red radishes, in the streets among the forlorn and the gentle or the radically misshapen and frantic faces, or it is raining and the streets are wet, shining and twisting like fish and the rain is splatting and booming upon the black umbrella and your heart is beating upon the sidewalk among the heels—or you walk into the great sad empty airport and it is late under the galaxies, do you not understand?

Quickly now, before the end, before the fade out, the utter dark, before the houselights go up, before the masks are removed as the clock strikes, before the figure grows small and regains the ignorance, becomes again the likeness, the cut-out, painted by a child.

PRAYER FLAGS

Nancy, we have walked far into forgotten mountains.
It is like a return, now: the moon-illuminated peak
that reaches unattempted into a black or a violet sky
at the distance where the actual merges with memory,
where one may speak from the real, like the actor from the mask,
the eyes immune to the wind
that shines against them . . .
For so long and on foot we have journeyed—

The cataract under the dangerous ice,
the birth in the animal shelter—
the aged, wrinkled, compassionate women with their several hands in the
       flashlight—
the steps twisting up, the wind
moving toward us like a runner down the snow . . .

In the attracting sleep we can hear the singers
each with the reason burning like a stone:
a cure, a knowledge, a reply—
climbing singly, slowly, the immense white
to reach, out of breath, the illumination at the summit—
peaks of rock, wind, and the callings,
the cries of the mad from their beds, who lost hold—
and those who stare through ice, who were released.
The row of prints follows the traveler across the dazzle
and a stringy, overburdened animal with frozen lashes.
Above us, a momentary monastery hangs,
the prayer flags shake as the wind possesses them.

THE MERRY-GO-ROUND

They blur, the interchangeable faces, mixing child and animal,
as roses upon the windstream,
the ceiling lights wheeling upon the painted shoulders, the manufactured eyes.
It is the loneliness that I feel here,
the gesture of recognition and withdrawal.

I write to you, from this table, simply, beside the white panes,
about the carefully turned and painted faces of the extreme animals.

Those for whom it is new,
creatures of the wheel.

Oh my daughter,
you depart, unaccompanied, into the instincts,
with the interchangeable children,
beside the animals with the lifted forelegs
or beside those great swan wings.

Our eye upon them like a luck
until the discovery occurs and they are incapable, for an eternity, of return.

I think of Orpheus, the moment that he turned.
Of Persephone stolen,
of father far as snow.

DOVER BEACH AT SANTA CRUZ

At Santa Cruz the children stare
Neolithic from the shore.
Seagulls hanging everywhere
Gray and aged as before.

I watch the slow, encroaching mist
Diminish their reality.
A thin and staring poltergeist
Helplessly confronts the sea.

Hostilities upon a stage
Quicken in my cranium;
Fantasies across a page
Illumine my delirium.

This gray, hydraulic scene exalts
A random, arbitrary cast:
The lame, the broken, and the halt,
The shadows whom the lamps outlast.

I looked to others for the clue
The key discovered by the few
Who lay upon the line their love
That we were, dear, delivered of.

The almost amphisbaenal mist
Encroaches from the Sea of Sharks
Bringing a chill where I exist
In deep, impenetrable darks.

DISLOCATION

I can articulate this skeleton,
examine it, and find it barren.
Lifting my lantern, darkly,
into the compelling maze
(the bats and the webbed wings)
I can enter like a shadow . . .

It is primitive, the discomfort of these bones
dislocated and enclosed in this
blue epidermis, and over which are wrapped
the green clothing in which I am distributed
bent here, the pencil scraping, writing to you
whom I locate in my brain, returning my stare,
whom I picture, there, like the luminous mute
where the planets are distantly positioned
in their delicate and centrifugal balances
directed by some strangely formed and knowledgeable
forehead, where the inchoate unconscious merges
into that dark, endless
drift of splendid minerals.

Swimmer, out of the darkness occurs
the momentary beachlong shimmer of white
and I have a reticence to accept or to accomplish
the identity that you have assigned me
where these loud, luminous
and incessant shores are the only buffer.

THE SAND JOURNEY

We adjusted the straps, like beasts—
stepped into the shin-deep sand, the winds,
the slopes of the dunes mingling like cloths,
the color penetrating the dusk like a dye—the distance—
the mountain like a hymn—

And the wind, days we cannot count,
and beside me you glimmer and shadow (the journey is double), the recognition,
our fingers through the wind—

And the circles of the sun focusing upon us like a lens,
and the eyes redden—one cannot open them.
Later
violent gestures, the falling upon the sand,
instinct—animals—shadows—the sand in the teeth, in the tins, the provisions,

How long, head into the wind, sand, an exodus, shadows only,
at the end of existence, beginning of dream—
I cannot speak of the limits, of sanity,
the loss of compass,
the delicate tremble and balance
upon the north, the thirst like a rage, animal,
the feet like a flagellate's, the round white eye,
the delusions
the emergence of unheard of ideals, the delirium, the terror,
the birds, my love

It is solitary,
seated at the page, to reconstruct the disintegration
upon the sand, an infinity away . . .
It was what was omitted, my love—
the journal—the journey out that we discovered to be plural—
I cannot fabricate
the dawn, in my skull, delicate, noetic, as a gate.

WEDDING SONG

1.

Bravest among us
dearest Molly,
enchanted and enchanting singer
receive a father's wish
that the dark be light
the crooked straight
the shelter wide.
That the bright branch blossom following the rain
that there be beauty in the winter like the peregrine
that the stone sing, and the stars answer.

So two approaching from great distances meet and wed
as when two dancers stand opposite, their eyes brightening with recognition.

I have these photographs:
The miracle first in the bright room
a mother's dark and lovely hair
how we became incredibly three . . .

Then playing the violin, the bow drawn slowly, loudly across
and the small repeating fingers
the rain at the window and the light upon the floor
the dark and beautiful concerto
and the clock in a shadow with its mind of gears and sprockets
striking some random, endless, unrelated hour . . .

These are shadows upon paper,
rapid footsteps upon previous leaves,
the world that is replaced
with your meeting and marriage . . .

24

Replaced by the actual and the aging
the difficult, only and human love.

2.

Let it pass among us like a shout:
the supreme logic of your meeting
in which I believe as one believes the dusk,
the nighthawk over the Owens Valley,
the mountain spring among the scarlet penstemon, the lupine and the eglantine,
lightning breaking its branches,
the tent at the cataract . . .

We drift on among the planets,
the stars like asterisks to some forgotten explanation,
drift across the algebra, the floating moons
and the far small galaxy spinning like a personal wish
that you receive the portion that is inalienably yours.

I watch you spread great wings
like the horses upon the mountain
when it is dense with stars—

and a family will applaud and weep and shout their love,
as when the dreamer receives the explanation that will release him,
as when one pushes out upon the raft, through the thick lake-flowers in
        the great light,
into the shining . . .

Molly and Lee
O reach with brilliant eyes into the completing garden.
"Ever wilt thou love, and she be fair"

ONE GROWS USED TO THIS

One grows used to this, it is the condition, these departures,
those for whom we have felt so much have wanted so much
for there to be language or meeting without fault: these departures,
diminishing upon the lines.

One grows used to this, the loneliness.
It is a puzzler, this isolation from all others
with whom we are locked like pieces
into position and motion, provocation and response.

I try to stake it out in the sands, an identity that is not theirs,
and I am left, standing upon the beginning.
And there is the mirage, if it is, ahead, in the wind
where the sun moves visibly through the sand and the wind like a rose
and sand is in the creases and the slits and the teeth
of the face, and the tears run long and glittering out of the dried corners
and I am folding, slowly, into myself, like a hand.

THE SURF SLIDES IN

The surf slides in as white as pages.
Another war returns to me,
Other shadows. Images.
I cannot name the enemy.

I search upon the sands for clues,
The ciphers of the past where we,
Disfigured by the mist, were two
Disengaging from the sea.

The shadow of the shoulder stone,
The ambiguity of gold,
The stations of the falling sun,
The moonlight on the dark Isold.

Articulate with inner speech,
Staring with the circle eye.
My intellect that cannot reach
Beyond the skin cannot reply.

The ceiling narrows from my sight
To shadow and the lettered doors,
To definitions of the light
Yellow along the corridors.

The ceiling light that stains the skin
Illuminates an older crime,
The shadow that I falter in,
The staircase I approach and climb.

I WATCHED YOU WALK

I watched you walk, unclothed, left-handed,
among tall birds solitary,
the dawn appearing like a shell. . .

It is primitive because
the tide is lifted—a shadow and shimmering—over the tracks
        of Aphrodite and the lodges of birds. . .
Pitted with passion and sorrow I lift toward a moon the mask
        that is also white and the likeness of death.
Thus I can write to you of the dream that is indeed the
        greater part of our reality.
Timeless are the forms . . .

It is to locate you like some bird within the fragile
        concentration
that I write to you. But there can be no delivery.

I watched you wading with long wings
among the shadows and the brilliance
an unreality that compels you without protest
and removal from which is age and wandering.
                                        I let you
from me into that shadow, stroke upon dazzling stroke,
like this fritillary, unable to struggle
from the limply green and compelling surfaces of the summer
        river.

3

LET US HAVE THAT MOMENT

LET US HAVE THAT MOMENT

Let us have that moment
before wandering into the matter of the dark.
The children pass in and pass out of our attention, and our door.
We pass them in crowds, they do not recognize us, nor we them.
We pass on the trail down to the confluence of rivers
and exchange a phrase.
The rivers are white, splashing, loud
and very fast, with small eddies among great boulders
elusive with the colors of sunrise.

Each turns from the other.
As the beam of a searchlight mounted upon a wall
pauses for a moment upon a face, then moves elsewhere
and the face is printed upon the memory.
So the thousand feathers of the wings
spread from the shoulders of a small, green, reclusive bird.

Enormous rocks hurtle through space, undeflected.
And a camera lens floating among suns
continues into a context of stars,
the rain of bright matter
where the new living pursue their existence,
upon legs like those of insects, and antennae
or arachnid lives upon eight swift legs across surfaces.
Or cells, in the margin of ponds, that multiply by division
to populate a very distant future.
And a ship with lights from nowhere pauses, as if to look,
and disappears into the wall of stars.
A gem-bright moon, whose planet is of broken mountains and waterless
streambeds. Our eyes create these.

And the incurious and programmed dead walk one behind the other
without song or want
and the scarlet shoulders of a thousand blackbirds rise
from the fields of children
like a dark weather across the sun.
I record the passage of time at my wrist
as I travel toward the forgetting.

A moon appears in the shape of a bright ring.

THE LOSS OF MEMORY

I have become reconciled to the forgetfulness.
The overtaking birds upon the unidentified traveler.
The reluctance to alter and the regret that accompanies the reluctance,
the dark, probable rose.

The room is uncertain like the spider's shining window.
Looking out upon the snow
across the squares and statues of the gameboard,
there is only the dissonance.

As if in preparation for an arrival, as if remembering
a promise of a return, a meeting,
not taken seriously, that now will occur.
The almost endless sequence of summers is about to conclude.

The loss of memory upon the mountain.
The wandering without pattern upon the snow,
misted unexpected crests and an immediate unlocatable bell . . .

Lord upon the mountain
I have not glimpsed the hanging monastery through the snowfall
in a moment of distance
where passage is unassisted. Is nothing, or is everything, revocable?

I follow the extinct figures that invented the firelight.
The unnoticeable bird at dusk like a small difficult word.

My heart will fall silent, that moment of inattention,
the last, instant, pointed stars and the unmistakable field.

DIRECTIONS

1.

Set out upon the incomplete journey
into lands beyond the wall . . .
Through the silence of the street approach creatures of the dream.
What is the choice? Tell me my choices!
The box and the shining therein? The disappearance in the cave?
The stone that I cannot locate? Successive lives?
Where do I belong?
With those who wait against the wall with extreme patience?
In the shadow beneath the overpass beside the infected stream?
With those who watch expressionless in the rooms with disintegrating
        windowshades
as the elms drift in a high, backward blowing, disappearing sky?

I wait for the knowledge to arrive beyond the forehead
like a small shining, like a bird's note,
for the stone to attract, the skies to part,
an envelope to scrape across the paving,
a leaf that I will recognize.

2.

My actions were determined not by the snow upon the black windows
(I write that I may remember you)
but by the small figure of grief on the pavement
out of Hogarth or Dickens—
the heart shining there like a cup—
who has gained some consciousness of the person
separated from all others—located in the drifting
rivers of disappearing stars,

unrelenting deaths and separations,
currents wherein he swims.

3.

In the rooms, the game upon the table, the idiot picture
shining and distorting. The silent angry old.
The lunatic necessities, the inability to communicate
or to discover the purpose, the "apology," the simple Why.
The utter uncertainty of the next conscious act.
As the man standing upon the roof-gutter, in the rain,
in the searchlight, above a thousand fists, and the shouting.
The old—like distant cousins—who will be removed
at some rare distribution of the stars.

4.

Stairs, rooms, mistakes, birds—
How can I convey to you the journey I am approaching?
I think now of ancestors:
faces that alter into other faces, the hanging hands,
shadows and firelight upon the animal drawings, the bison, the earth
        beneath us.

The street, Nancy, narrows. The horizon comes nearer.
The tortoise climbs back in to the sea, great shell subsumed by the
        darkness
beneath the scarce gleam upon breaking waves.

THE LIMITS

The shelves are in deep shadow.
An occasional title glimmers like thin gold in the sands of a stream.
The colors and abstractions woven into the carpet upon the floor
by an aged weaver or child, in remote sands, in the shade of a tree.

Your eyes glisten, is it the light?
A wind is blowing into the room from the lifted window.
Tired, you are seated at the table, in the light, your hands,
opening and closing the book.
Your eyes are dark with the mysteries,
you said, that have no solution, as a dream
or isolated memory.

You place the book with the green binding back upon the table.
The limits have come closer.
The elaborate frame of golden foliage
within which the painting of the child emerges for a moment
from the darkness of the background, as emerging from a past
or from the Mystery to which we will return,
like a messenger waiting for a reply, unaffected by time.

THE STATION

The huge iron, stamping upon the tracks, the flames under the engine,
the bolts, rods,
the loud steam out of the wheels,
the dark dust they shovel in, the gleam of shoulders,
the blue, roaring door.

The breaking out of dreams, compulsively into the consciousness
I cannot control, and the train trickling down
across the map that I have folded out, the long, diminishing, lighted
   windows into the dark.

Arrival under brilliant glass, the great ceiling, the press of hands, people,
   teeth, clergymen,
the disguised and the grateful,
the doors opening, the stairs let down, the baggage wagons, it is you
behind the faces, in the letters of the signs, among the wraiths
in the steam beside the great wheels, whom I could not select
for a moment could not discover—

glass and iron and steam, those who emerge into focus, have, for a
   moment, expression,
motion of the eyes, asking a direction,
which train, a destination, and withdraw, resume
the confusion or panic that contains, at least, the pattern of the search.

I am alone. I cannot fabricate
the progress into the wind, squinting,
looking for the recognition, the identity,
   twisted and painted, held to the face
before the unmasking galaxy, interminably slow.

THE STATION 2

The past we chase. A train moving out. Great blasts of steam,
great wheels, gradual at first, out of the station—
glass, iron ceiling, and steam dispersing.
And a ridiculous figure who runs hopelessly, helplessly after
an untraceable past.

Those whom he loved were so briefly present. They do not look back,
they being of the past. As he slows, without breath,
perhaps stumbles, catches himself, and turns back slowly, reluctantly,
disbelieving, in a confusion of loss, death, memory, tricks
and falsifications of his time.
                    What is it they take with them?

Returning to a vacant, waiting present, the numberless clocks,
A station with all trains gone.

WHO WE ARE

I cannot continue this betrayal
of those who speak out of simple deception, exaggerated pasts
(they shout as through the loud bars of the cell)
who people my dream, populate my eyes
interrupt my wishes by an incessant calling
the shattering telephone and an indecipherable answer.
The challenge to duel, in a clearing. The antique pistols.
The white mists of earliest morning upon jackets.
Seeking each the ending of the interminable story.

It is the children. Starved or sold.
The converted and the crippled keeping underground, intricate caves.
The orphaned in the fields of explosives.
Sunset unremembered upon inaccessible mountains reaching into the snows.

I think of those animals who lived on land, ancient,
now unseen, uncounted, with eyes luminous and amber
under the skin-fold. They know their paths.
They know without sight the presence of the enemy.
Of old Jerome, canonized, in the engraving,
his fingers tapping in meditation upon a greatly staring, unearthed cranium
from the centuries, lacking dreams or wrongs.
Of John, staring into his dark night
that approaches from the surf like a bride.
A preternatural reality illuminating like an eastern sky
Teresa in her cell.

Do they mean nothing, those moments?
The faulty lighting, the stage ropes, the scenery
the curtains pulled noisily across, shadows upon the velvet,
the house lights and the laughter?

At night the statues climb out of the sea, and crumble to the sand.
It is the madness that I sense. The terror
in the garden, in the room.
The sky is eliminated over the street.
They will return into their memories, the paths into the woods.
Where they will encounter their deaths.
They are masks lifted upon poles.
They are with me, their never-closing eyes.
The mirror reflects the dark weathers of a word.
Do you? Do you too change from the living to an undisclosed location
like simply changing flights?
The sun upon an almost endless aluminum wing?

ALL THAT IS FORGOTTEN

1

What brought us—what brought us to this surf
bringing, from the distance, the accidental brightness
toward us upon the sand.
Our speaking in the silence and the silences of our speaking,
because it passes so quickly, as we pass
into the increasingly luminous, those vast rotations
from which it will be no longer visible,
the moment that reaches to the heart,
as the rapidly repeated feathers of the iridescent bird.

All that is forgotten I revisit, standing, unnoticed.
All that is forgotten, but that attracts us like the North, the white North,
a word that comes for a moment into view but is ignored and disappears
into the distances, the concealed trails,
other locations, those ancient hand colored maps
unsearched of cloud, rainbow, the patterns of migrating birds,
a meadow of cobwebs at sunrise, shining and distant,
the crag from which we stared into the dawn.

The past is a fast-changing garden. A collapsing of time.
It is the window where Edith waits,
staring at the bright unbroken line.
A gallery I visit, with the lights on, of sculptures shaped
by pressing, discovering hands. A language
of all that is forgotten, ignored,
but that attracts us like the forms and the necessity of love.

I have no words to find you.
There are not days remaining in my years.

2

There are always attackers. It is always unprotected.
Those crossing the field with torches and crosses,
or the armies climbing up from the sea
bringing the goddess, serene and implacable, out of the dark of the ships.

I have visited the mad in their gowns
upon whom the door remains closed.
It is fear of their noticing, their speaking.
The unexpected ferocity of the one who so sadly stares,
so bruised by her captors, who will change into a dove.

Think of Persephone, taken.
The underground coronation among the radiant minerals.
Demeter, obsessed, in her despair or madness
hurrying across the earth with a gray rain.

The cripple lifts his cup toward us from the dust, O Lord.
The heretics escape by rope who will be suspended in cages.
The lifted, braceleted arm of the priest at his office.
The worship, upon the steps to the river, of a mindless derelict,
skin and cloth and with the paint upon the forehead.
The excited, untranslatable speaking
as the waves lap and gleam upon the steps
reflecting the motion of the mountain,
the wavering columns of the temple,
and the wings of a cliff-swallow.

DISTANCES

Little light is left.
At a great distance, bats rise out of the earth
or temple abandoned, without pilgrimage, to the roots
and great plants, an endless and beautiful rain.
Bats hanging or relocating among the beams of the great ceiling
over ancient images who receive no reply.

There is the attraction, ecstasy even, of the dark
incalculably deep vortices of spiraling star-matter,
the shimmering theorem,
rivers glittering through inchoate space,
and the galaxy on the edge of which we walk,
this darkness and the attracted heart.

Now the surface of the stream reflects vertical willows
that are lightly shaking. The pond is for the swifts,
with the thin, green iridescence out of the sky.
Or the goatsucker's erratic directions.
The ten thousand insects that move or hover, together,
over the pond-gleam. The green intelligence floating
at the edges, or fastened to water-stems;
and the snake a silent swimmer.
And we, in the late dusk, diving through the green-silver surface,
into the attracting dark.
We who find our biographies in the long trails of stars.

4

CHILDREN'S CRUSADE

QUESTIONS

Who made this? Who brought us to this past?
Are we a function of the passing of time,
motion and emotion?
A Creator who remains out of sight in the mosaics above the arches?
The master-spider with his silks, like jails,
located in a dark interior?
The priest waiting with raised arm at the top of the nearly vertical steps
in a shimmer of green feathers of rare birds
and the gleaming wings of flies?

A trembling pope at his window
displays upon his finger the stone that renders him infallible
the faceted stone that dazzles like our eye.
He watches from his cerements
the heretic who disagreed, who will not answer,
and those who stone him.

Why do we choose to fill the sky with just this god?

THE DEATH OF THE NUN

And the Nun walks, in her great black habit, alone,
through the corridors, archways, stairs
to which she committed her brief presence,
accepting the changes that must occur
upon a hopeful, almost transparent face,
the Latin increasingly difficult,
and the causeless tears.

She mutters as she walks
and shines, to the passerby
the green glittering of her glances.
And she enters her introspection
like a gate in a wall.

Hair, beneath the white hood
once yellow, now gray
as the mist from the ocean that the wind blows in fragments
across the beach, sand, the great, tubular, floating sea-plants,
the white, sea-worn wood, the flies,
the mist that obscures the houses whose windows, only,
shine softly through.

She enters the vast stone space into the full blazing
of the stained glass
and in the great airy transept
from the concentration of the light, the doves descend,
birds, she was taught,
created from that light.

CHILDREN'S CRUSADE

And I think of those children upon that single and longest journey.
Their joy as they think to approach some eternal field,
a promised pasture, a change of breathing, a heaven.
The cross, that star, like the key to the gate
to the sky.
      Bringing them instead diseases of the limbs,
deceit by clergy, the woman beside the road at her dancing,
the invitation, as in a dream.
Hunger. dust, contraction and the stillness.
The birds, out of the sky, adjust, with apparent patience,
the wings upon their backs.

The sad survivors. Others possess them.
Capture and sale,
the usual negotiations, a handshake,
lips sliding back upon mistaken teeth completing the smile.
The cages of a caravan, the children, ungrown, captive,
to labor in crops and stalls, or selected for worse
who thought themselves children-saints
whose likenesses would be placed in the niches
until that certainty, the Day.

And the wind brings down the temple, the stones falling
into the grass, an extreme rain, an assertion of power and anger,
the violence, masks depicting madness, the crowding rodents, the flea,
an ancient sea, overturning ships, sails, and the rowers,
the hooded helmsman.

And all that we must bear of our stammering,
failures, evasions, causes, consequences, all of the past
that is withdrawn from streets, schoolyards,
the dark holds of shuddering, leaking freighters. . .

We follow like laughing children
some piper in his greens.

THE INQUISITOR

The aged, infirm, over-robed Inquisitor
bringing his dialectic,
the street emptying as he walks,
striking fear where he directs his sight.
Here is the seriously believing priest
keeping to the Law
putting the torch to the kindling,
and who contradicts him will perish
in the swept streets
his robe the color of the wings of the cardinals.

The Questioner, by the act of questioning, is incinerated,
the saint, conversing with some point of light overhead,
an unapparent thing.
He struggles and is quiet.
The heart flames in the wind.
falling, out of sight of the legally saved,
and still falling,
beyond sight or hearing of the Spheres, and the cities.

GAUTAMA

And another cave we heard described by priests
of the river called sacred,
a violent river with trees and leaves
shading an entrance
from which one might survey the kingdoms upon earth
and later, an evening of brightly similar stars.

The Prince (for he was of a royal line)
seated himself in the position
his fingers touching the earth
and began his great silence.
And the dancers, and serious speakers,
that were sent to show him, to display for him
an alternative path of a higher truth
underwent a change to a thousand shadows of a thousand leaves
and the noise and sunlight of the passing river.

The enemy has slowly fallen
and cannot again rise.

THE BRIDGE

The dark is another place we know without guides.
Walls, furniture, seem closer.
We feel them with our hands.
We know
where lies, in darkness, the other place.

We can see the bridge, massive, wet, in a thick mist,
enormous before us, which as children we walked upon
evading the endless cars of the terrifying freight train,
huge and growing larger as it approaches us, as it gains speed,
bellowing, shedding black coal-smoke in great clouds
from the entire length of the bridge, or trellis,
into the ravine, with the creek, a refuge for many,
and into the clear air breathed in
by the many souls hymning there.

THE FISH

It is the Fish. Of the old stories.
There are the scales of a gold hue, as in your painting.
For you too have seen him.
The obtruding, prognathic jaw, eyes that must see,
fins lovely as scarves in motion
as the water changes its flow.
It was known to Inkidu as he swam deep.
It was observed by the Sumerian Astrologer,
swimming past him into the sky.
Survived the furnaces of Bel.

Known, it was known to the ships.
To the fabled fishermen of the Pacific, setting sail from white sands.
(So sacrificed to the sea-wind, and the rowers did not turn back.)
To Magellan as he fell in,
to Drake in mid-ocean. To Prospero by his singing sea.

To the followers, with the paint upon their foreheads
descending the steps into the slow, green, sun-lighted Ganges
it became a language.
The real fish passes them. To them a symbol.
They speak of Peace, hands together.

Fishermen throw, as one,
the deadly hooks into the sea, attached to long shimmering lines.

THE CLIMBERS

I have the window-view of far, pale, moon-illuminated mountains.
It is a trick of the light, or a modulation of a dream.
Small figures are visible crossing, one after the other,
the lavender and shadow of the snow.
Preoccupied, they do not communicate
beneath the immense myths of stars and the moments of the past.

They will begin the climb. The wind like a shout.
The distribution of food and drinking water—
the tent in the snow-wind, the distortions of the fever—
illumination, madness, and medical attention—
the frozen lashes and the dazzle upon the face,
(the rare snow-violet)—
the dark, amorphous and attracting sleep—
the loud pass and the remaining steps,

the arrival, like a terror. The great wind. The Chorale roaring.

THE STONE

The stone—toward which all passion and quests are directed—
love, it rests, simply, upon a crude ledge within a cave
in some immense, unidentified mountain wall—
a range of violet and light, of rare and adamantine minerals,
a Urals of goat trails and sunrises.

Hideous to many, it will resemble the bag of black leather left behind
in his bewilderment by the gentle physician whose eyes as he
departs fill and glisten, who lowers his head, raising his arm to his
forehead.

And in the great hall, delicately ceilinged, where the rain-light shimmers
through the many panes of the windows like Isadora floating
among the scarves, it is the unmoving alabaster of the Roman
brow.

It is the seventh of the difficult encounters.

And where the archer of the legends lives alone—in a doorframe, in the
pine mountains—aged now, wizened and amused—it is the
shadow of a fish moving upon the luminous pebbles . . . It is the
luminous shadow moving upon the deep pebbles.

5

THE UNADMITTED

SERVICES

A green hillside. The sheep in the floating fog
come softly to this pasture
unworried in the ragwort.
A creek is lighting the alders.

A frog is motionless, noticing,
and the quail with the single feather and the black rings at the eyes,
and trees, still bearing, flowering, ancient apples that the light splays through,
a disused boundary fence, the green remaining stones.

Is it a memory then? A novel put aside?
Now that the birds speaking in those branches are intelligible to us
and the unusual colors of the field?

In the empty, dark, unvisited house
with disintegrating windowshades and a broken porch,
actual, sad implicating figures are calling to us for rescue.

> Edith watches from the shadows of the room
> into which she, once beautiful, retreated
> looking out of the sea window at the gold line on the horizon,
> Edith of shadows, when the sea shines like a bird . . .

Partitions of the dark. The maze.
The nights sitting over this typewriter among the attracted insects in the
electric bulb.
Reaching the kitchen, the blue flame, the web at the window, the
dazzling faucet . . .

And a sister taken ill beyond imagery or penitence,
Susan, in the green ward.
Susan, an assumption I can no longer hold,
the voices intensified with secrecy speaking the word cancer,
your gentle hands.

You located the small door, and we entered into the foxgloves,
the garden-leaves, the hedges—the Magician who alone held power
the far white deep-robed figure
here, behind the tree, where we look, where the jay stands.

They are captured, or quickened, by moonlight, these
eternally repeated people, in the stage-ropes and the sceneries
that are disproportionately in shadow.

John, always unreal, leaving no prints in the sand, finding
equations chalked dramatically across his cranium
I first saw among the shimmering architecture of the glassware
filling the laboratory, in his white robe bent over the burner in
        utter danger.
Who went by rail and lift to the sanitarium in the snow
who entered, after the electrical shocks,
into an eerie madness, his small eyes looking
this way and that, occupying halls.

Barbara, tall, betrayed, her endless contralto—
standing beside the piano, upon the carpet pattern, reading the
        libretto—
who became a wanderer with her child.

And Paul, whose great French dramas with gold folding curtains,
        the audience rising tier upon tier,
remained unwritten. Paralyzed.

As when the string broke upon the dark wood of the violin
when the bow was drawn down and across, in mid sound,
and the whole shimmering concerto was gone, replaced at once by the
        actual corpulent
figures who were seated with expectation upon the loud chairs
and who move now, in conversation
toward the glass doors and the darkness beyond, containing
        stars . . .

The darkness and beauty that seem to be simultaneously present
in each and expressed by each gesture, look, reply, as the light
reaches them—Jim, Paul, Ginnette, Barbara, all of them,
the loved and those not loved . . .

THE UNADMITTED

Those who lack the clearance. Who did not receive the letter.
At dusk when the proportion of darkness increases
and the sun is completely red
and the bats climb out of the earth or out of the old temple.

The guilty, the living
those who weep, the mortal,
those who can see, those who can read, taken from their door,
the crippled waving the crutch, the very tired
have been roped off, not admitted.
The dead on the beachhead with their never closing eyes
The starved dogs in the heat of the street. Unadmitted.

Those who dive for coins
the traveler, the betrayed
the seeker with his misinformation
those who live at night, hidden from the light
the mother of the story
the slow, uncertain, hesitating old
those who live in the imagination of another
the Devil
the somnambulist upon his roof-edge at night
the worshipper from another country
the two children staring at the sea

Hunters and gatherers
accountants
those who are ill and not yet ill
the guilty, the living

the furious monk hurling the inkwell
Chief Joseph
Ishi

They lack clearance
have been roped off, edited out
not admitted.
They do not have the letter.

Those who draw the bow splendidly across, and are abruptly interrupted
who had been waiting for the interruption
those who, in their caps and gowns, are abstract as the star-combinations
that govern or define them
John, in the goatskin, eating the live locusts
Jim, Horst, Barbara, Cornelia, Paul, Dave, Robert
Lord, entering the subway, the great, tiled, bottomless depths,
the screech of rails.

EDITH

At the attic window, the single occupant staring from his thread, a noticing eye;
tables, chairs—twisted shapes that the light does not reach—
waists and gowns and military uniforms, the attracted moth.

And a painting from your period of storm,
a sea black without a sky in the unglued frame
lies forgotten in the illiterate webbing.

You once were recognized and spoken to by others.
Ran beautiful upon the cliffs below the great lighted sky,
beside the vast, shining subsidence of the sea upon the sand.

You are seated, without conversation, in the unusual light of the room,
at the window that is possessed by the spider,
waiting, as the clock advances, for the moment to reach you, again, out
        of sequence.

The meeting on the beach, the surf recapturing the moonlight as it folds,
the accident at the gate—under the great wheels—

The child escapes, or returns, looking back as if for reassurance
into the repeating past.
Attempting to remember,
in concentration to recapture that which, forgotten,
continues to attract, to compel approach, like a scruple.
Climbing long stairs toward a recollected room.

Edith,
darkness approached you like a wrong that you had willed,
whose memory is a stone,
singing like a cricket beneath completely familiar stars.

61

MARGARET

The furniture is motionless and recently occupied.
The clock continues to strike,
(the hands mechanically advancing, that reach and release
each momently dazzling number),
the leaves have entered, lightly scraping, across the
        floor.
The stars occupy the doorway. The rememberers
approach across the field.

Margaret—you walked beyond the reach of our sight
with the noticeable limp, beneath the instant stars.
You walked, unassisted, beyond the gate
beneath the huge evening-gleaming trees
where the moon hangs like a bright nest in the branches,
the thousand leaves moving upon the air—

The mountain-outline that you described as reaching into your sight as the illness
        progressed,
and the gate and the mustard-field,
a rapid and clouded sky and drifting trees,
a distance beyond your strength,

Oh single traveler with slight shoulders.

The loud door and the light upon the porch—
the shout and the interrupting trees—
whom we searched for—whom we despaired of—Margaret—

The egrets, Margaret, will return, white as pages
in the darkness, shutting great wings,
until dawn brightens the windows, reaching the beds of the rooms.

62

THE COLLECTOR

Dear Carla,

My guilt is great. I cannot find a perspective
in which to view or to verify my presence.
To stake it out
against the comers—those approaching from the past, those preparing to appear.
Through the distortions of the window-glass
the collector waits at the door.

A sound of a bell reaches across the pre-war field.
So the castle swan moves upon the sky-reflections
and you, distantly remembered, upon the bank
approach in the glimmer and wings of the insects
your foot in the medieval flowers of the grasses
increasingly real as you approach—out of courtesy, a kind of love . . .

Failure. Placed in the stock before the starers in the street.
The blue wrists. My heart that will fall.
Replaced at birth, my blood doesn't match.
The madwoman left me, in my disproportion,
in exchange for her theft. Returned into the trees.
Thus the madness I take into the streets with white hair.

Morning. Small misted cobwebs are spread shining
over the seldom-gleam, the shadow-rustling, of a stream.
I watch a colony of bees swarm (like an engine) into the
        apple branch
the sun shine like a small pearl through the Mendocino mist
and the birds that will be destroyed are returning unaware.

PAUL 1

Your letter to me I will answer now:
there was a sorrow that we thought to speak
and that I never did, but you somehow
could write it out beneath the skies' mistake.
Where did the path divide, the birds depart,
the stars go out? Decide that we were wrong?
The shadows grow on lives we did not start
and yet there is a triumph in your song
and you through brightest windows now seem tall.
We follow out the lives we would unlearn,
you sing to us from branches when we call,
from empty drifting houses you return.
Too late to speak, I only can recall
the shining words you wove before your fall.

PAUL 2

Who seek the beauty that is only given
the livid flame released beyond the bone:
by accident or anguish they are driven
as Paul upon the porch that night alone.
There would be causes, dark mistaken nights,
a father's horses or a brother's stone,
some visitor to your expecting sight —
O the stars are thick above the field you own.
Return from your horizons whom I call!
although I do not think you will reply,
a solitary traveler, dear Paul,
your letter like a window to the sky
brings back the human necessary song
to us for whom the stars are faint and long.

AN EARLY DEATH

I cannot find the page wherein you first found some definition
where the discovery occurred that is you, the first description.
Dusk gathers against the yellow wood of the floor.
The first crystal hangs, dazzling, over the field.
Algae on the stone, and your name by which you were identified
briefly, briefly. Under cover of darkness now your forgotten name.

I have no words to find you where you are.
I cannot find the moment that you were.

A wave falls, like the great initial verb, crushing upon the sand,
scattering like your countless pages the moments you were saving,
waves and the winds of the enormous, unpublished sea.

JIM

Jim, I speak to you now, after your suicide, among the black windows,
      in the night-dream,
in the awful moment that is located in a small lighted room,
the white bulb upon the ceiling cord and the unmistakable shadow
      against the wall,
the doorway that you occupy with noticeable hands.

I believe that the dead speak and that I may speak to them,
shadow and bone and paint, at the turn of the passage.
Incomplete voices, incessant picture images . . .
The suicides approach with their lamps and accusations
across the red, extreme abstractions of the carpet.
And your face separates insanely from the unawakened,
comes with examining eyes.

The sunset painting that you had left, not yet dry, against the wall,
the great vowel upon the sea-horizon, and the scarred sky,
and black birds that flock with the wind-changes,
that possess the branch.

I think of your capitulation in a lighted room above the wharves,
the pilings and the black repeated waves,
where the light does not reach. Not permitted to return.

HORST

After your death, Horst,
I found your painting of the figure brought back
from your dream, whom you lost even as you reached,
the light as though a door had been left open.
Many are the distances needed to complete the figure
of the room, and of her. Some move and change
as the window changes and a river appears.

We share, you said, a complicated dance-pattern
in black space. A confusion of deaths and of dreams
we share with all departing things.
I watch a climber returning from the snow, small
and growing larger toward me.

Return from your memory, Horst, that white mountain.
The hands of the damned raise as if to be heard.

DENNY

Denny,

Whether our acts occur as consequences—willed or beyond will—
the necessity reaches out of the dream, the static pattern:
as the somnambulist climbing out upon the roof-tiles,
as the light plane meeting the wall of the mountain-ridge (the sudden
        unecognition),
as the stranger approaching beneath an abstract, stained and
        unmistakable sky.

Last year, remember, the glow of the low faint field,
the sage that we walked through, shoes upon the plants, the goatsuckers
streaking the sky, the first bat at its flight out of the earth—

Now you stand beyond the light, not entirely actual.
Moments, disparate and urgent, reach you, out of sequence, again,
as you watch, in meditation on the manner of your death.

Was it archetypal? Out of the sky?
The priest determining from the star-positions the fortunes that must follow?
The madwoman upon whom the dove descends?
The madman who cries out, and again, as he paces
room after moonlit, unoccupied room? What is it he searches?

The traveler has reached the river on his journey to the far night,
the suspension bridge, huge and wet and still.

It is the last day, and the electricities of the sky have begun
striking first the temple, the pillars, the sculpture, the memories
the Place of Skulls—
the figures on the crosses who are no longer speaking,
where the few women wait, together, in the immemorial grief, with small
        shoulders, like birds.   69

RUTH

I remember Ruth, hooded, the stars at her shoulders, bringing in the darkness her mystery to the edge of the land.

Reaching the termination of the journey. Train, ship, taxi beyond the gate, on foot—to wade, at the last, into a dark surf scarcely folding, like silk, upon the sand, deeper as she wades.

The sun-reflecting windows of the long train moving silently out across the untested trestle, intricate and immense, above the gorge from which mist rises, a habitat of reptiles, snakes, outlaws.

The freighter, of an unlisted registry, dropping suddenly into troughs or lifted upon enormous crests, the shouting upon the deck, the light of the portholes, submerged—waves that reach a prodigious, an exalted height, and deeply subsiding—random destruction—motion—meteorological anarchy—organ noise—and the uninterrupted human cry of contraband in the loose links of the chains.

The unlicensed taxi before dawn, with a great engine noise, through narrow streets, between dark windows of perhaps inhabited rooms, across the bridge with the balustrade and lamp where the woman waits for the actor, into the badly lit sections beyond the river, of cast off furniture, handmade fires, careful conversations, cardboard shelter and a lightly falling snow.

To the sand at last, the lifting hills of wind and air, beneath the extreme unstarable sun, shoes pushing back into the dry sand, among the tracks of small animals and of native snakes.

To swim, at the last, out from the shore, beyond the reef, stroke after splendid unhurried stroke, with assurance toward no island, beneath no repeated cloud, leaving her own small very brief wake upon the rescinding sea.

70

THE LAST LETTER

I do not care, winter coming on, to continue the sad posture,
a figure abandoned, for a moment, upon the curb,
to avoid or perhaps to select the accidents and the disaster,
the dreams of great rodents . . .

So much has been removed from me.
I thought to awake you, there, in your wings.
I thought you would return to me, I thought what if years
if distances intervened. But I am left in a room
whose emptiness I am unable to describe or to convey to you.

You who stood there, within the door,
your hair dark as violas, to receive me into these rooms,
the sunlight upon the woods, are gone like a forgetting.
The space once occupied
is now unoccupied, the motes striking upon the surfaces.

All night watching the farces,
the old injury, the rose, the betrayal,
the prophecies beyond the limits of our notation.
But they are masks upon a pole, pushed up and down in the procession,
the saturnine, the great grin,
the white and silly and mindless, that grow and crowd and occupy my eyes . . .

One cannot dream again. One cannot walk into the photograph. One cannot alter
the consequences of surrender.

In the deep trees, the birds, jostling, singing, adjusting their wings,
the amber, the forest bees,
the butterfly like a dark leaf, the tree whose great roots
enter into the grasses of the earth . . .

71

It is the muscles of the lids that ache, pressing together.
The dancer waits among the shadows and dark foldings of the
            curtain
for the light and the violin.

OLD SHIPWRECK

Grandfather, after these years, in your old desk
in the drawer with the letters, love kept hidden,
your unreliable map with dolphins mid-sea,
the compass with the various norths,
great winds issuing from the four corners,
beaches like white promises,
the location of the conversion to the cross
that will overcome Satan.
And in a northwest corner
a lightning hangs over a high-breaking, whitening sea
the momentary lightning of the dark waves,
erratic paths of electrons that strike
the masts and cabins
of the breaking freighter.
The wreckage will be pulled by the sea-storm
into the huge, enormously rising, spiraling
waves that create the vortex and voices
of the sickening, possessing center.
All ropes, ladders, the vast tearing of sails,
the food from the shelves with all the organisms,
the bottles of forgetting and temporary lapses,
of harm and Happiness,
the rodents, struggling,
the hands fallen from the yardarms,
the gunwales.
Others, with the small,
drowned in the hold.
No living thing survived, no rescuer attempted salvage.
The captain unseen and his rumored companion.
It was a disappearance. It may never have occurred.

LEAVES AND BIRDS

Condemned to occupy a cell, you paint upon the walls
a likeness of jungle, of vines, a dense rainforest.
A washbasin, porcelain, chipped, provides the sounds
of waterfalls. Brilliant half-seen birds.
The window through which the barred light enters the room
is beyond your reach. You receive your meals
From a woman in guard's clothing. The wall remains concrete.
The leaves and birds are to your vision real.

It seemed, you had said, that completion
is strange and rare. Incompletion, dissatisfaction,
the resulting near-madness are the unexpected necessity.
So when you faltered and the brush fell, your jungle incomplete,
the incompletion, looking back, becomes expected.
The frame in which you, we, lived, died.

A Michelangelo chapel occupied by a single, dying worshiper.

6

HOW IT INCREASES

BATTLE PAINTING

The mystery, refusal, defeat, is always.
As your painting of one of our wars
is a mystery. The cast of wounded, shouting
and the dying.

Not the armored horseman on whom the light gleams
blindingly, but in the faces vanishing and calling
who will reappear, if they do, in, say, a dream
or there in the room centered in the huge canvas
placed there by the intensity of grief.

I think of the dispossessed. Armies across the plains.
Friends, traitors, masked assassins
shadows slipping within shadows.
The temporary people,
voices soft and threatening the death.
Dancers calling from beside the stream.

In the vast white gallery, under the lighting,
your painting of one of our wars, or is there only one?

DYNASTY

Responding to the camera
a child on his elephant
and his loose, fluttering colors and silks
(a certain confusion of words
disturbance of understanding).
His the stunting air that we share
the air that is golden with the far waft of petroleum.
He brandishes, with help, the great family blade.
It is the signal for the shooting of the guns
and thousands lie dead, or twisting, upon the fields,
the sands, under the fallen stones
or cry out from a mind that has broken loose
possessed by the desert terror.

Darkness. Of the mind as painted by Goya
or drawn in charcoal.
Lightning into the sand
lightning breaking like far branches.
Thunder and father's wrath.

THE MUSEUM

I have paced the museums, I cannot recount to you the number and the variety,
squinting upon the flocks of sheep in the beeches, the water upon the wheel,
the pear and the pearknife upon the cloth, the great twisted gold foliate
frames about the little dark idiot oils.

Or it is the tapestries, my dear, that are smothering us,
superfluous, floor to ceiling, the pathological needlework,
the immense moths,
the conqueror—the boar—the nuptial—
(and the weavers—blind—pensioned out—in their shawls—
under the harsh stars)
and in a dark, low-ceilinged room, the bed of a bald queen.

I turn, push, the heart immense, through the startled, the critical, the clothed,
out toward the dazzling approaching exit,
make the descent, like a teal, pedaling down into the shadow-world,
the point of the spiral, the fish, the box, the beginning,
rejoin you, stand
upon fibula, calf, and the blue and bifurcated veins
among the hats, the wet folded umbrellas, and the shoes.

HOW IT INCREASES

It is not the moon after moon above an unending jungle,
the cave entered sideways between rocks,
the gods lighted by running water.
The carving on an altar,
the sacrifice of dogs.

It is not the ritual in the quarry, the lunatic sacrifice.
It is not the warrior beneath the face-stripes
and the threatening feathers
nor the vertical steps to the narrow platform
for the volunteer-victim,
preceding the others, to prepare the paths of the paradise.
Nor the bats who will depart the temple in thousands
with their great ears.

Not the steps of the church with the weeping woman
or the immobile hands of statues spread in the gesture of the Benediction
or the billowing Pentecostal tent pitched by the river
nor the Believers leaning forward from their folding chairs
in their carriage clothes, and great layered dresses,
speaking, singing in tongues.

It is what Goya saw, how it increases, the cruelty, the immensity,
the cry into the eternity of space, for ever
explosions of seas against rocks,
small moons with the beginnings of life,
planets with their turbulent sands.

THE HORIZON

It is the sadness that rises from the pages like a scent of the air we breathe
because below the horizon hangs
the thick, nearly unbreatheable air of the city
the twisted effulgence of the depleted planet
the detritus whose particles float, breathed, among us
and petroleum runs in flames over the pavement of the street
and the horizon burns.

And you imagine, you imagine that the great, still-visible eye
is fixed upon us, risen from the far, fallen and vanished
civilization, a culture of light,
where the convicted, the captured, the depleted, the solitary
lifted stone to place upon stone,
to erect with defeated backs
a simple, ample temple
beneath the heat and the great weight of the sun.

A culture of stories, caves, mystery
priests that climb stairs to guide the sun in its measurable arc,
the great fixed eye looking out over the future,
our city, and us.
                    Eye that stares across millennia, through
the shining dust. Desert cruelty, and the brief but intense and private love.
The doves group and speak together up in the interstices of the architecture.
The articulation of the stones.

Captured, driven under the lash, caged, like the cowering
cats. Those defeated in the desert wars,
the lame, the halt,
cry out, and those captured, in their flight, with skillfully cast nets
or the false ground they fall through, to the bottom of the pit.

Nothing remains. Not a bracelet, a sandal, an earring upon the sands,
but the great fixed eye looking out over the future,
our city, and us.

APOCALYPSE

The car stopping, upon an instant, suddenly in front of you,
the earth tremor that too is a manner of speaking,
the field parting immeasurably deep that the elk cannot cross,
the tree that the wind brings nearly to the ground,
the great black lettering in the newspaper rack,
the madness that spreads and spreads upon some light wind.

Those who disagree
are left upon the chair or upon the floor
or will join the loud repeated steps
behind the colorful, wind-blown, heraldic banners into the field—
the thousands pushing against thousands,
tank treads in the loud thick mud,
the slow sky-filling brilliant explosion . . .

And the immense, dark planes lift, one after another
from the asphalt, between runway lights
into a gray fragmenting mist, a great wind,
to gain that altitude above the countries
above the warehouses and the railroad centers
and those living their lives carelessly in the street-lights.

And those who fall into the dust, whose heart stains through the shirt,
bleeding into the dust. Forever there.
The television distracting from the corner, gleaming grimly.
The great impenetrable indestructible machine with tractor treads.
The racket of the helicopter propeller blades in grassless lands.

It is a vast vacuous rhetoric that imperils us like a vortex.
Clouds illuminating a city of columns and whitened citizens
of statues upon white steps, and the derelicts,
the likenesses of senators, of stucco over a wire frame,
the unusually thin dogs in the streets,
a public clock upon a white wall,
the hands already moving
rapidly toward twelve.

THE DELUGE

In the museums I return to that massive, dark, over-framed painting of
      the biblical flood
that howls across the rooms, a wind, a demolition—
it is a fury, like a prophet, a loud half-idiot jeremiad, a damnation of souls—
like that at the streetcorner, finger pointed as in the poster—
it is the verb left out of the language.

Souls—that cling with small hands, with fingers, to badly painted rocks,
beneath the terrible God speaking with repeated brilliance out of the sky—
or they float, mere swimmers, with ineffective strokes in the chaos of
      lifting or utterly disintegrating waves—
or floating among the chains—
souls staring with round eyes out of the comical deluge, calling to rescuers
(and will
until the paint crumbles upon the canvas)—
to rescuers who themselves, small swimmers, have been pulled into the
      vast, insatiate, twisting spiral of the sea.

Together with masts, spars, all, the handpainted half-clothed smiling figurehead,
the little rodents,
and the great vanquished statue of Bel,
the emaciated carriers of the stones,
the particular colors of fallen gardens,
the terrified horses of Babylon (detail of an eye reflecting light),
and the armies unable to swim, helplessly lifted upon the flood . . .

On the right, and distant upon the waves, and growing smaller,
Noah floats with his animals.

This dark, overpopulated deluge.

Punishment. Beneath the lightning and the electricities, one erratic bird.

It is a painting without a miracle.

There is little sky.

NOAH, AN EXPLANATION

And if I fall back before what appears distant and immense,
    a mountain on the plain, a ziggurat,

And if I appear to reconcile myself to the black and countless birds,
    the absence of shadow and the increasing unfamiliarity of those
    few remaining abandoned figures who bear with them no hint of
    identity or thirst, who contemplate in their meager coverings like
    pilgrims the directions and the distance,

You must—(do you not?)—sense the limitless despair, the mourning
    beside the certainties, the little fixities, the numberless lunatic
    necessary acts,

And the dull, unrequited need to measure, to build with hands and
    syllables, among daughters and the morning, among the wings
    and horns of the animals,

From trees, the hull that is lifting now out in the rain, upon the
    encroaching tides.

7

THE FLIGHT OF THE MONARCH

THE POOL

The pool under the butterflies is green. It clings like cloth at my
      ankles—the white-leaved willow, the boulder—
I can see the yellow wing of a vireo move in the margin grass
and I can view the desert moving without water in the valley heat.

I draw breath into this luminous skeleton that I cannot reconcile.
climb up to the ledge,
granite among the scarlet starflowers and the million audible bees, and
      dive
dispersing the water reptiles and the floating dry insects
into the kinesis, the eclipse, out of the calendar
among figures of grief, half in shadow, their intricate organs of vision
floating out—fastening upon me like an answer
chronicled upon the broken tablets.

I do not know what insanity compels me to this admission.
I write to you
the identity I had with so much difficulty managed was withdrawn
where the hanged man stares back without recognition
and there is a face, abstract with rage, inarticulate and flaring
and they are performing the opening statements of the Toccata and Fugue
and I recollect with sorrow
your forehead wrinkled up, and the eyelids shutting
with great force one against the other
and the priest working at his clues
the old murder hanging over him like a star.

A sky of dark and fossil speculation, mineral and extinct,
        the long mist drifting across,
the feeling inarticulate of stars and the skeletal traveler.

It is to make myself plausible that I lie here,
the wind among the grasses, the eyes lidded.
Chrysalis among the grasses woven
bringing us into the family of all breathing, migrating things.

PETROGLYPHS

I remember—or there recurs like dream across my eyes—
a cratered and a volcanic country
and the shoes pressing upon the dazzling dust
and the shadow stunting . . .

The lightning upon the desert
the electrons illuminating the huddling primates
the animal trails we followed, through the rabbit brush to the light of the water
the gleam and blue of the dragonfly
and the little, yellow, mortal birds
in speech upon the stems.

The carvings I discovered
scuffed by birds, struck by the desert meteor,
effaced by rain and lizards,
by day the violet and deadly ray . . .

A calendar that has gone into the spiral.
I recognize lightnings,
antlers, the hand.
                            It is beyond the place
of such extinction, shadow upon granite,
that the symbols cross my consciousness like clouds.

I cannot placate the hawk
among the little dark luminous eyes
of the weak and high-pitched animals
the snake upon the sand spiraling and unspiraling . . .

The tears glitter
into the dust and the creases
of the face, and the lips crack,
and the sun is a blue, blind, burning stone.

And the delirium spreads like a dazzle,
and giftless the eyelid lifts, and the emerald selects
and all that was plausible
has been replaced by what is real.

THE RESCUE

The white, violent wings twisting randomly upon the sea's surface
crests and the valleys where the freighters are lifted
bows pointing skyward
and the survivor on his raft with shirt for flag
and the fishermen who will not return to the village above the cliff
where she stares and the child stares.

Some rare vortex spiraling
brings us into the much older culture, society, civilization
far beneath the sea.
Gossamer the gracefully moving wings of the fish
that surround us. Their eyes are round.
Fixed, unlidded eyes, and with a glimpse of gold.

Thousands turn, as with a single mind, one word spoken
take flight into an invisible distance.
Another, with but two dimensions, wanders without interest
beside an antique hull with rowers still in place.
None speaks audibly.
There emerges from a fissure
an animal with great intelligence
uncoiling its eight, living limbs,
with skill and quickness it changes its location.
Above us, the surface of the sea gleams
like sliding plates of glass. The sun shows
like circles expanding within circles
and the hull, the keel of a freighter
breaking into the great houses of the sea.

A hanging keel. Rust, flaking
bos'n and mate staring into the sea
a geometry of angles and lengths of gold rectangles
so hanging from the sun
upon and under the salt-surface
the light reaching through the interstices of the sea.

A long fable-thin ladder lowers from a silent winch
lowered for rescue, foot and hand.
We remove ourselves from the length and positions of the remaining drowned.
We rise above their circle
break through the surface of reflections of the sky,
of great unlasting white and blue petals
and seeking hands.

STILL

Lightning illuminates the room
and a figure standing.
The piano like a great shadow.
A mirror suddenly observed,
a great yellow flower.
The stone shines upon the table,
the syllable.

The room is beyond time. Is not in time.
The voices growing louder
conceal the silence
intensify your presence.

I stare into the past lives, and the guards are upon me.
I see the enormous sea that preceded this desert
and the animals upon the boat, Noah navigating by the star.
The dead of the wars stare and call.
And the sand-hills darken
and the sky is stilled
over the halted river.

FLIGHT OF THE MONARCH

Dark butterflies in the cypress forest
pause in their solitary migration
hang from a giant cypress
clinging to the tree and to each other.
They hang like a great shadow,
their wings for the moment still.

Together, they are like a lantern hanging in the forest darkness
or the gorgeous fantasy of an imprisoned madman,
like a cloth requiring years and eventual blindness
to weave, sew and knot, a material
woven in another country of inaccessible villages.
It is like the message left for rescuers while the sender weakens.
Like the wings of the queen
waiting upon the tree for her legions, her swarms.
An enormous, dark, mysterious, rustling thing.

They will separate, one from the other,
in thousands, thousands, those small lantern-wings.
This insect creation, insect instinct, a display.
And there comes to them the sound of slow swells, rising to crests,
that fall back, exploding, white
upon the black-green ocean
(and a minuscule freighter moves endlessly upon the horizon).

A small thing, beating its butterfly wings, seeking
its beginning, wings ragged, the loss
of the dust of color. The splendid black
and lantern-amber, mere wing-remnants.
This pause before the morning.

After this flight, near death, why? What
is the reason? Is it love and the perishing
as salmon do, climbing without hands?
Into the falls, into the cataracts,
with the single urgent purpose.
Climbing vertical walls of falling water
evading the birds, and the great dark bears.

THE BOX

This box with the lid and lock has been given to me to bring.
I cannot remember when, or how, or if it was begun.
Or by whom. Perhaps I carry my ashes
and I am unaware that I am no longer in your sight
within the radius of light. Like a lapse of memory or perception.
Or attention, because the wind rises with
the movements of lights and leaves against the window-glass.

The box secured by rope, the box with the lid.
The mule, the dust.
Wading the rapids. The key is lost.
Heavy to the jungle-porters, traveling single file
beneath the hanging snakes and the small wings.
Heavy to the Sherpas of the snow.
Thus it is carried to the destination.
There is an impairment that accompanies the possessor, a lapse, a loss.
Mortality is sighted in the great walls
of white, difficult mountains, that reach
to what is held in awe.

I do not know what the box contains.

All boxes contain insects.
small black markings, exoskeletal
with legs, the face of hardware,
its eyes seeing all that is evil and that flies.
A brain with nightly episodes
of the one, terrifying dream, forgotten
infinitely small.

I think I carry these with me, and will always, in a simple,
black, cube-shaped box with a lid. Through foreign streets of narrow eyes
the hidden arsenal, the jackal-like attention.

I carry the night.
I carry the universe in which I dwell. Perhaps it is the Thesis,
the solution, the reality-changing proofs before which those great
rare minds light up like wicks, like cathode tubes, in a forest darkness,
in a universe we cannot share.

The apparently empty box, it contains
a universe we occupy, one of countless,
in the box by the physics of capture.
It will be short-lived.
It is of stars
galaxies, suns in their orbits,
planets in theirs,
planets of falling bombs and rifle fire
seas, ships and fantasies of always.
It will die, but like the Insect will produce
another and it another. (Will we know them?)

And the microorganisms from that subreality
which, as if they plan this together
will cause that last day
for which so many wait in hope
for this will mean vengeance
following the message of the last chapter.

Unburiable
it is being returned to its birthplace
the salt-sea caves
among the brilliant sunlit wave-spray
and flocking shorebirds.
(In such beauty she grew.)

Lift the lid and you are stone.

FAR FROM US

From seas of misting, strangely combining chemicals,
the air of poisons,
ancestors carrying these memories
and of very deep, gently swaying gardens,
the heat from the furnaces in the fiery rifts.

Animals dissembling to resemble others,
that take on the colors of where they are.
The shadow-stripes, an animal's back in the still savannah.
Scales of great animals attacking to eat.
Enormous trees hanging over the carnivorous woodland flowers.

What did they bring with them, those travelers, into our fields?

And the great sculpted stone, a head (a chin, nose, eye)
fallen to earth, broken, possessed by vines,
And the pharmaceutical roots of rare trees (roots hanging into the caves)
the rain in the loud leaves.
A butterfly upon deeply blue iridescent wings rises from a water-stream.
The flowers, petal, calyx, and stamen, devour the clicking insects,
deceived by color. And the temple destroyed
by growth of trees and the knotting roots in the steps,
the threshold of the jaguar and the threatened snake
and the stone-destroying leaves of the golden lichen.

And we watch ourselves, at a distance,
standing, hands joined,
upon an endless beach, with the rare shells,
and the kelp abandoned by the tide, and the small birds,
those runners after the surf, and the never-before-seen sea
with the random glittering. We remember instants
of light. Far from us now. Far as children,
far as we were.

ABOUT THE AUTHOR

Fred Ostrander comes of an old California-Nevada families. Three of his great-grandfathers arrived in the state in Gold Rush days. One herded sheep in Yosemite and gave his name to Ostrander Lake and Hut; one made a fortune in Nevada silver and San Francisco real estate and lost it all in the earthquake of 1906; a third stayed put in the city and ran an antiquarian bookstore, a few volumes from which are the pride of the poet's shelves.

Ostrander was born in Berkeley, graduated from the University of California, married (a classmate) and raised four children, and founded a successful business as a commercial real estate appraiser. The other pole of his life, from boyhood on, was Yosemite, where he backpacked many miles in the company of his father, his wife Nancy, and later of their children. As mountain lovers the Ostranders were drawn to the greater ranges of Asia and made several trips to Nepal and Bhutan. These experiences, together with his sailing with the Merchant Marine in the Pacific during World War II, pervade Fred Ostrander's poetry.

Ostrander developed his poetic skills in the circle of Bay Area teacher/critic Lawrence Hart, a grouping sometimes known as the Activist poets because of their credo that poetic intensity must be maintained throughout a poem. Responding to his early collection, *The Hunchback and the Swan* (Woolmer/Brotherson, 1978), the review journal *Parnassus* found his voice "odd" but "invaluable to contemporary poetry because it sharpens our perspective about possible alternatives to prevailing . . . modes." Ostrander continues to share his poetry and counsel with like-minded poets in what are known as the Lawrence Hart Seminars.

Ostrander's poems have appeared in sixty or more publications and were recently showcased in *Sulphur River Literary Review* and *Nimrod: International Journal of Poetry and Prose*. Since 1995 he has been one of the three editors of *Blue Unicorn*, a respected all-poetry journal now in its fourth decade of publication.

Fred and Nancy now live in Walnut Creek, California.

Printed in the United States of America

Breinigsville, PA USA
18 September 2009
224327BV00002B/1/P